ARTFUL DRAWING FOR KIDS

By Margaret Carson

E mail: mcarson8888@comcast.net

www.yourart.com

Publishers: Amazon Digital Publishers

Library of Congress No. 2021901914

U.S. Copyright Office,

Washington, D.C. 20559

ARTFUL DRAWING FOR KIDS

BY MARGARET CARSON

TABLE OF CONTENTS

ARTFUL DRAWING FOR KIDS

Hi Kids! If you like to draw, we will get started right now.

DRAWING MATERIALS

Let's begin with the basics. You don't need a lot of materials to get started.

A few pencils, ...with not too sharp points, are best. Some white paper, an eraser, and a ruler and you're ready to go!

You may already have all these things around the house.

...and you may try to use an easy flowing black roller ball pen to draw. But remember, with ink...you can't erase...yikes!

If you can't find a ruler, you can always use the edge of a greeting card or a book.

We won't have to use the ruler to measure most things, as it's mainly to use when we need a very straight line.

DRAWING MATERIALS

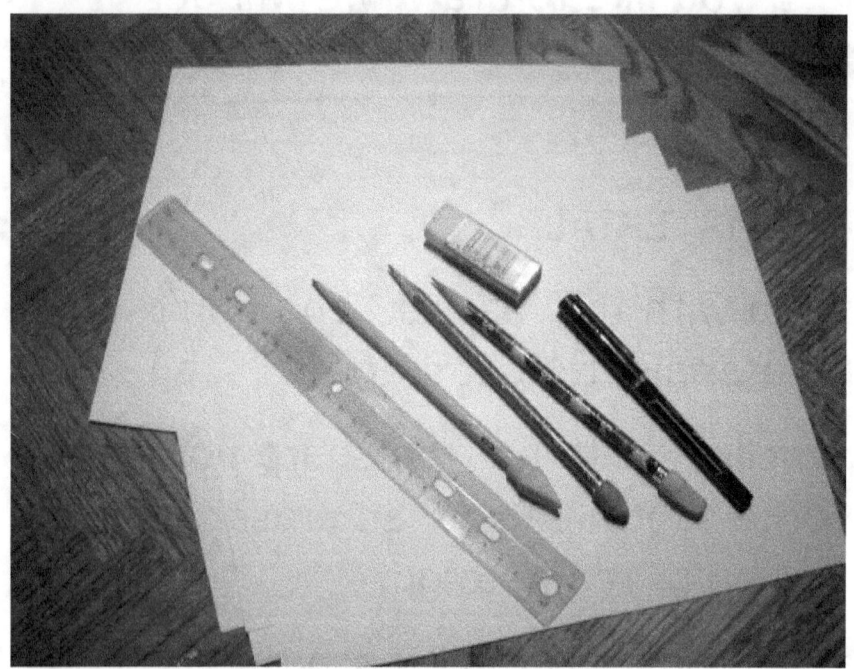

Drawing materials:

2 or 3 Pencils

Eraser

Ruler

Sheets of white paper

(You might use a roller ball ink pen (from $ store), but be careful,…it won't erase.

NOW LET'S BEGIN TO DRAW!

HOW TO DRAW BAMBOO

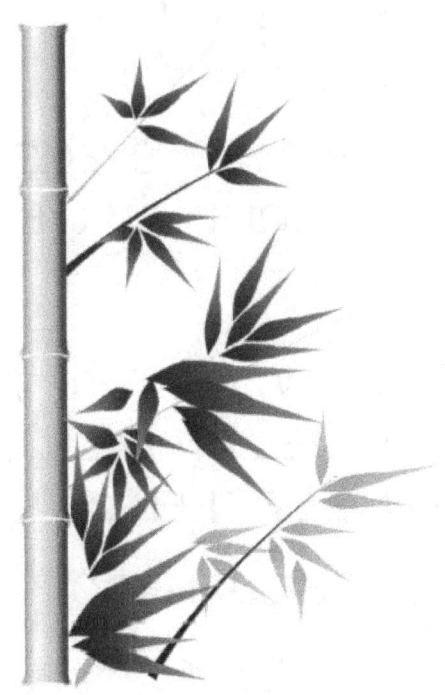

Here are the 4 easy steps to drawing bamboo.

- USE A RULER OR STRAIGHT EDGE AND DRAW THE 2 LINES FOR ITS TALL, THIN STALK.

- NOW DRAW THE TINY BUMPS OR GROWTH RINGS ON THAT STALK. CAN YOU SEE THEM?

- DRAW THE THIN STEMS COMING OFF OF THE STALK, (SOME CURVE A BIT.)

- NOW DRAW ALL THE POINTY OVAL-SHAPED LEAVES ON EACH STEM...AND SHADE SOME OF THEM...

YOU DREW THE BAMBOO... WELL DONE!

* * *

TENDER BAMBOO LEAVES ARE WHAT PANDAS LIKE TO EAT! THE LEAVES ARE KIND OF SHAPED LIKE SMALL OVALS, BUT

WITH POINTY ENDS! DID YOU KNOW BAMBOO IS A GRASS, NOT REALLY A TREE.

WOW! I HOPE YOU ENJOY DOING THE DRAWINGS AND THAT YOU LIKE YOUR FIRST BAMBOO DRAWING A LOT....

At times something you may see may be hard to draw or...sometimes its easy to draw. See the 2 Pandas. One is easy to draw. You can choose the one that is best for YOU!

LET'S LOOK AT HOW TO DRAW PANDAS...

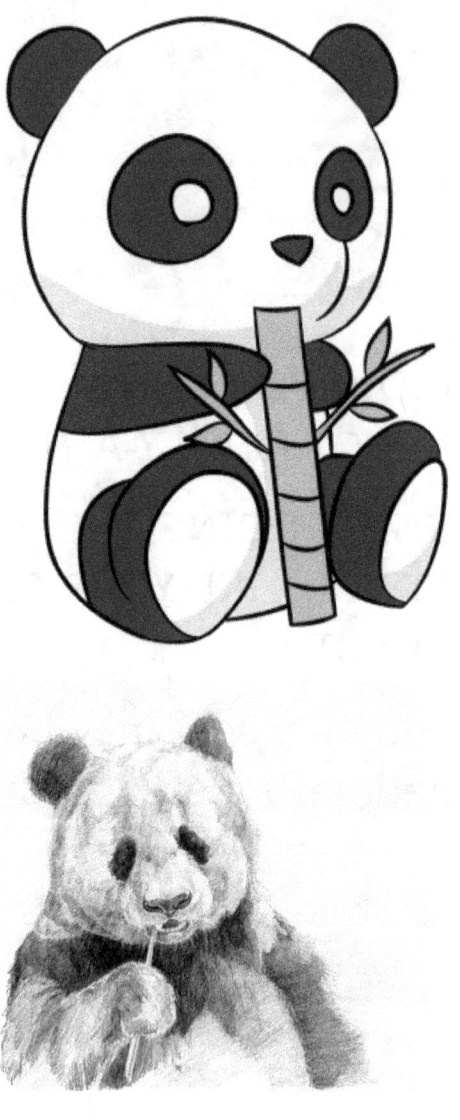

- PICK ONE TO DRAW

THERE ARE 7 STEPS TO DRAWING A PANDA

- IN PENCIL DRAW A CIRCLE FOR ITS HEAD.

  (USE LESS THAN HALF OF THE PAPER FOR ITS' HEAD...AS YOU WILL NEED PLENTY OF ROOM FOR THE BODY).

- DRAW TWO SMALL FLATTENED CIRCLES FOR THE EARS.

- DRAW ITS EYES AND NOSE. LOOK FOR A MOUTH, AND DRAW IT...ADD ANY TEETH , IF NEEDED, TOO!

- DRAW THE ROUNDED SECTIONS OF THE BODY

- THEN DRAW THE ARMS & FEET

- NOW DRAW THE BAMBOO STALK FROM THE BOTTOM UP TO ITS MOUTH.

- NOW SHADE IN THE DARKER PLACES ON THE PANDA BODY.

If you liked the challenge of the 2nd panda with lots more shading, draw it using the same steps as above, but add lots more dark and light shading...then use your eraser edge to remove some shading for 'fur-like' and whisker details! A handy tip!

... YOUR PANDA DRAWING IS DONE! NICE!

* * *

There is an ancient Chinese art of drawing bamboo plants. Some artists spend their entire lifetime painting and drawing only bamboo. They become very expert at it!

Could you draw one thing for a lifetime? I don't think I can... So let's look at drawing a flower next...

This will help with observation skills...the art of looking really, really closely at something!

DRAW AN ORCHID

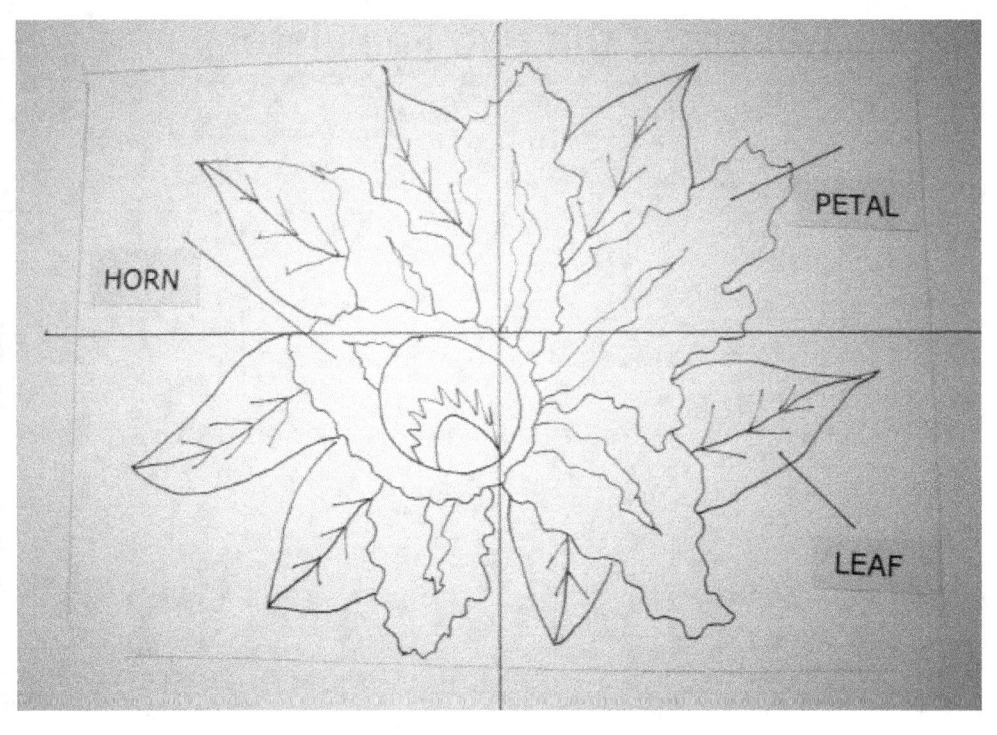

DRAWING THE ORCHID – 7 STEPS

- IN PENCIL, LIGHTLY DRAW ONE LINE UP
THE MIDDLE OF YOUR PAPER, and ANOTHER
ONE ACROSS THE MIDDLE.

... THESE TWO LINES MAKE YOUR 'GRID'

(...you will erase the two lines later)

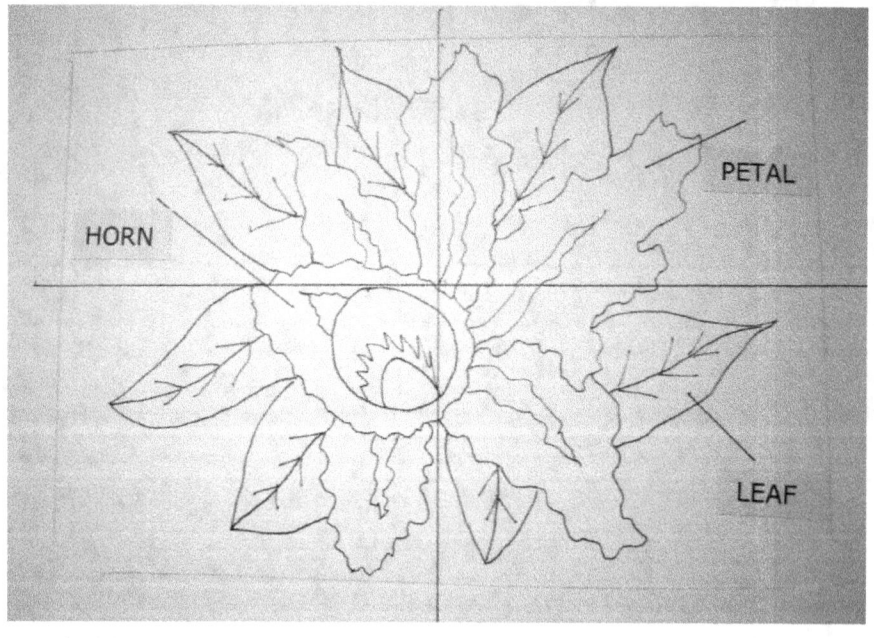

A grid on your paper helps you put things in
position better.

- START IN THE MIDDLE OF THE GRID LINES

- IN PENCIL DRAW THE HORN...IT'S IN THE ORCHID CENTER,... & THEN DRAW A SEED POD INSIDE IT.

-SEE HOW THE GRID SHOWS HOW TO PUT THE 'HORN' IN ITS CORRECT LOCATION...

- DRAW THE CURVY HORN LINES AROUND IT

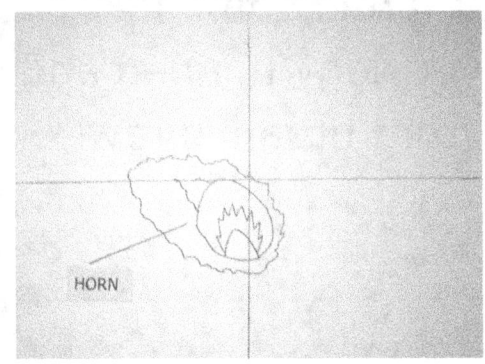

- NOW DRAW THE ORCHID PETALS AROUND THE HORN. I SEE 5 OF THEM.

- LAST, DRAW THE 7 LEAVES...(THEY ALL HAVE A SEAM DOWN THE MIDDLE).
NOW YOU CAN ERASE YOUR GRID LINES.

THE FLOWER IS SO PRETTY! GOOD JOB.

HERE IS A DIFFERENT FLOWER BLOOM

IT IS IN THE MODERN STYLE OF GEORGIA O'KEEFFE, A FAMOUS ARTIST. She is well known for her simple yet larger than life paintings. She was very ecology minded and wanted to save nature from urban sprawl !

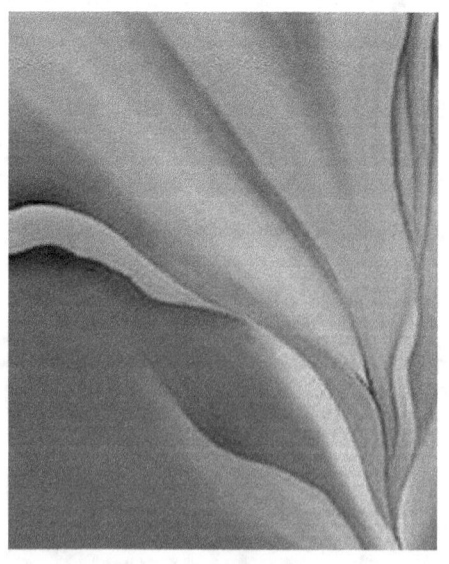

-DRAW IT BY STARTING IN THE BOTTOM OF THE HORN AREA.

-THEN DRAW IT FROM THE BOTTOM UPWARDS, PETAL BY PETAL.

-YOU CAN PUT AS FEW OR AS MUCH DETAIL ON IT AS YOU WISH. USE NO SHADING IN SOME PETALS AND LIGHT OR DARK IN OTHERS! OR MAYBE COLOR IT IN!

-USE YOUR ERASER FOR MAKING STREAKY BITS! YOUR MODERN FLOWER IS DONE!

WELL DONE YOU!

* * *

DRAW A RAIN-FOREST FROG

YOU CAN DRAW IT IN JUST 6 EASY STEPS:

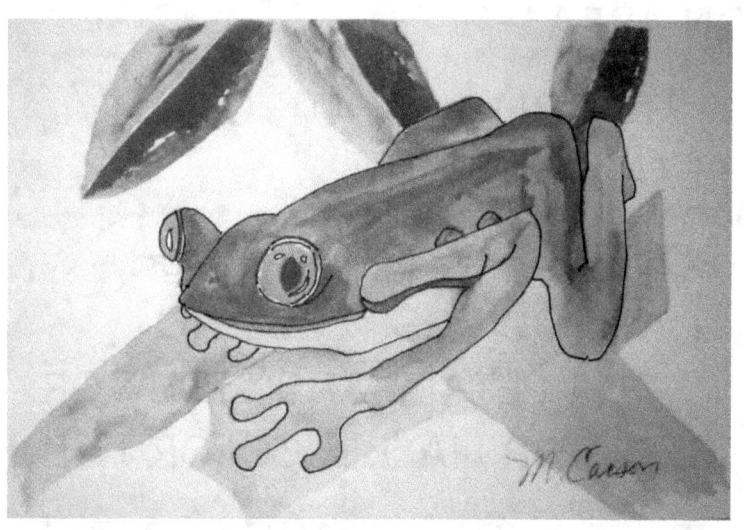

- USE PENCIL TO DRAW A CIRCLE FOR ITS BIG ROUND EYE. PUT IN THE SHINY BITS.

- DRAW THE TOP OF ITS HEAD... THE POINTED NOSE, AND ROUNDED CURVE OF HIS BIG MOUTH

- NOW DRAW ITS OTHER EYE ON ITS 'STALK'

- NEXT DRAW THE TOP OF THE FROG'S
BACK...ALL THE WAY TO THE LEGS

- THEN DRAW THE BACK LEGS. (ONE LOOKS
JUST LIKE A BUMP). ERASE IF NEEDED.

-NEXT DRAW HIS FRONT TOES AND A LONG
FRONT LEG, AND HIS OTHER TOES.

-THEN LIGHTLY DRAW THE BRANCH HE IS
SITTING ON & THE LEAVES AROUND IT!
VOILA!

WELL DONE YOU!

* * *

YOU CAN SEE HOW ADDING SHADING TO
THE FROG MAKES THE PICTURE SHOW UP
BETTER. HERE ARE SOME TYPES OF
SHADING DONE WITH PENCIL:

HOW TO USE SHADING:

- PENCIL SHADE GRADING CHART:

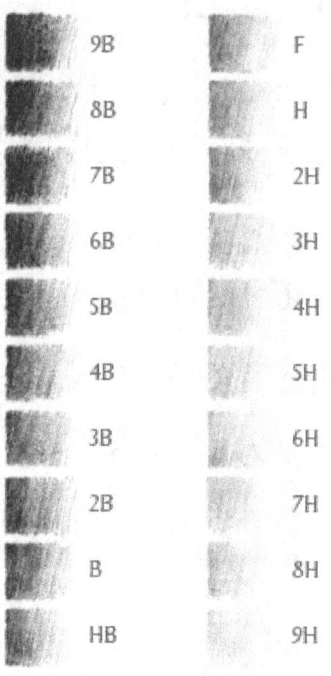

9B	F
8B	H
7B	2H
6B	3H
5B	4H
4B	5H
3B	6H
2B	7H
B	8H
HB	9H

A very very dark pencil 'lead' is called a 9B; and pencils with softer graphite 'lead' are 2 B to 9B. Pencils with light shades are all 'H'...I believe it stands for 'Hard'.

A set of 20 DIFFERENT drawing pencils will give you many shades of graphite, and advanced artists often use them.

ABOUT PENCIL SHADING

A normal yellow school pencil is a medium shade of graphite, and is called a 2B. See it on the chart.

You do not need to buy a pencil of each lead type. You can use the 2B yellow school pencil by pressing harder on the paper with a 2B for a darker shade...But it will be hard to erase if it is very dark. Use the pencil lighter on the paper to have a faint shade.

Shade is important in art when you use a shadow for a certain effect. See how the shadow of the apple makes it look more important, more round.

* * *

DRAW THE APPLE IN 5 STEPS

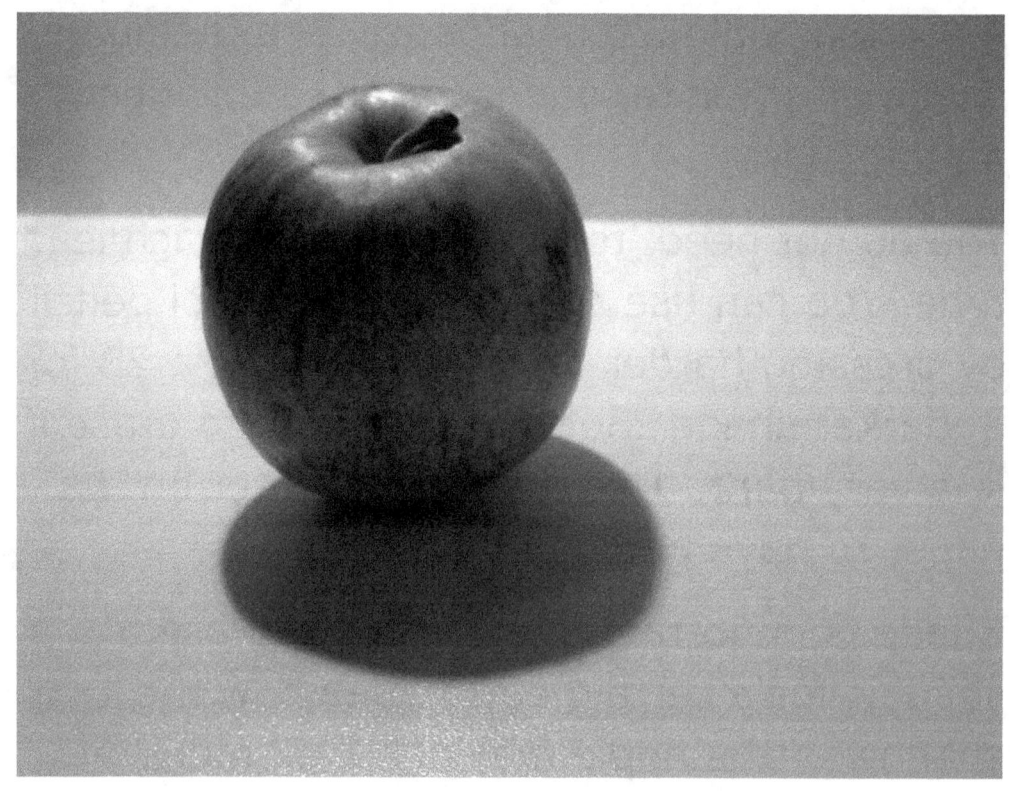

-DRAW A ROUND CIRCLE FOR THE APPLE

-NEXT, DRAW THE BIG SHADOW UNDER IT...

THE SHADOW IS ALMOST AS IMPORTANT AS THE APPLE ITSELF! IT SHOWS UP BETTER.

- DRAW A STEM INSIDE THE TOP OF THE APPLE

- DRAW A SHADOW UNDER THE STEM AREA WHERE THERE IS THE 'DENT'.

- FOR EXTRA EFFORT,   IF YOU WANT TO GIVE THE SHINY HIGH-LIGHT AROUND THE TOP OF THE STEM AREA, USE A LIGHT SHADE OF PENCIL STREAKS AND CREATE THE 'HALO' OR SHINY CIRCLE AROUND THE TOP OF THE APPLE!

OR YOU CAN ALSO ADD AS MANY OF THE DOTS ON THE APPLE SKIN AS YOU WISH!

WELL DONE!!

* * *

TYPES OF SHADING

An artist often uses different types of lines for shading...

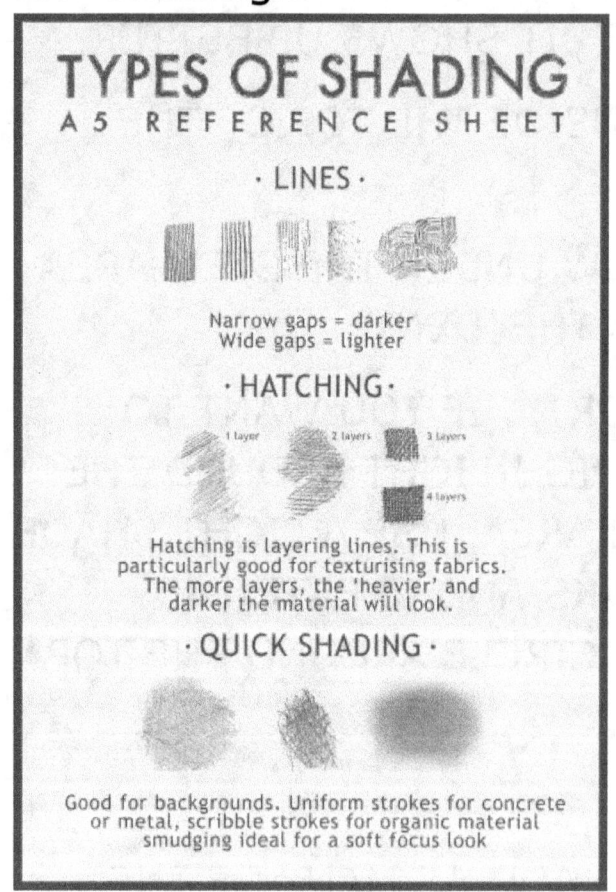

When you draw the hibiscus flower next, use some dark shading to make some areas stand out! Try shading with your 2B pencil.

DRAW A HIBISCUS FLOWER

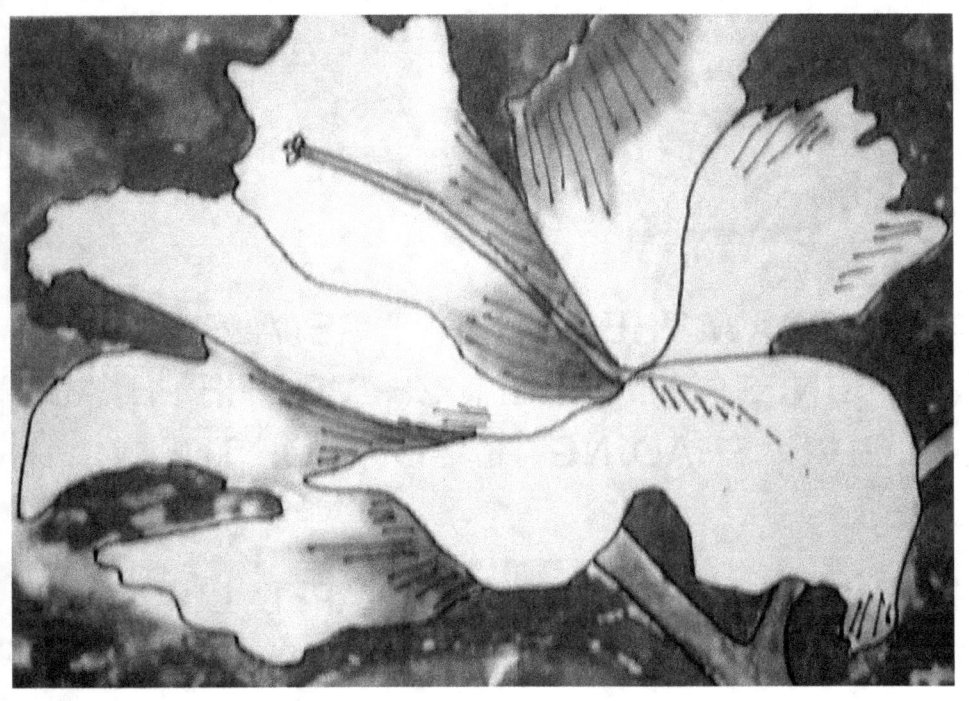

- BEGIN BY PUTTING THE LONG STAMEN- IT LOOKS LIKE A BENT STICK- IN THE MIDDLE.   IT HAS 3 SEEDS ON TOP.

- DRAW THE PETAL THAT THE STAMEN IS SITTING ON. ERASE TIL YOU LIKE IT!

- THEN DRAW THE 2 PETALS NEXT TO IT. (...they all connect in the center)

- NEXT DRAW THE OTHER 5 PETALS, & ADD 'dash' LINES...THEY HELP SHAPE THE PETALS AND GIVE SHADING TO SOME OF THE EDGES.

-LAST, DRAW THE STEM SHAPED LIKE A 'Y' AT THE BOTTOM. NICE HIBISCUS! NICELY DONE!

* * *

DRAW A FACE

Next we will see how a man's head and a lady's head differ. Overall, her head is more tapered and graceful; his is more wide and 'chunky.' I suggest you pick just one of them to draw first.

HOW TO DRAW A MAN OR A LADY'S HEAD

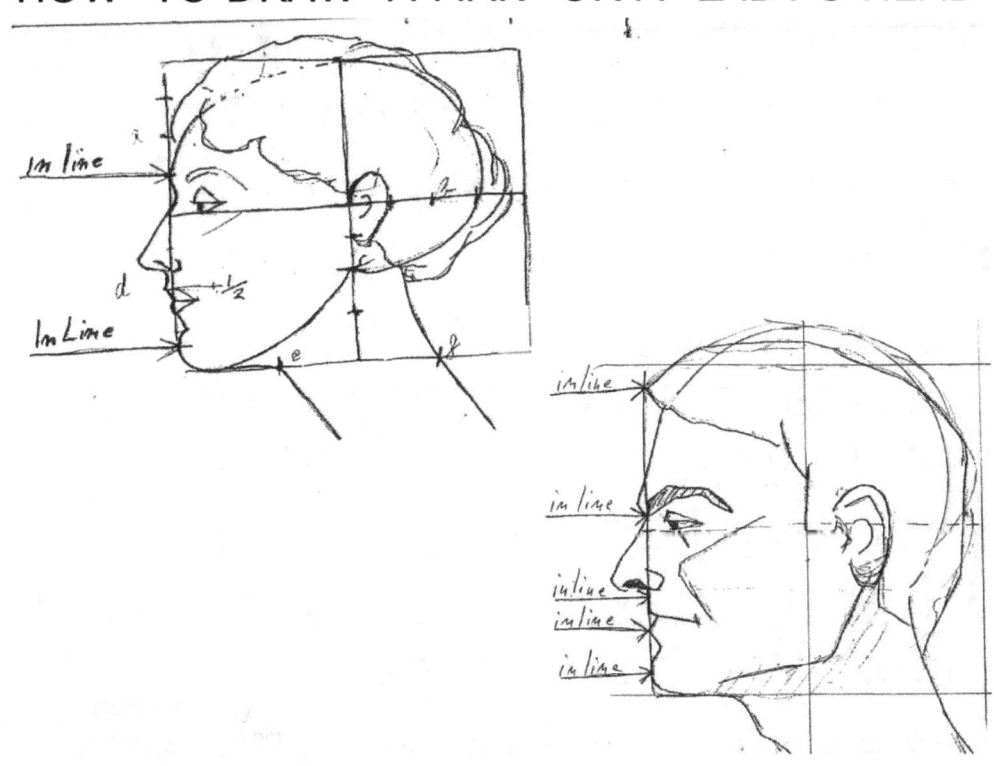

THERE ARE 8 STEPS TO DO A PERSON'S HEAD...

- DRAW A BIG SQUARE BOX. USE A RULER OR A STRAIGHT EDGE OF A BOOK, ETC...

NOW MAKE A 'GRID', BY LIGHTLY DRAWING ONE LINE UP THE MIDDLE OF THE BOX, & ONE ACROSS THE MIDDLE...

WHY DOES A GRID HELP YOU DRAW, YOU MAY ASK? A GRID HELPS THE ARTIST PUT THINGS IN THEIR PROPER LOCATION...

SEE HOW A WOMAN'S EAR IS ON THE GRID LINE OF THE SQUARE,

(BUT THE MAN'S EAR IS FARTHER BEHIND IT AS HIS HEAD IS LARGER... SO HIS EAR IS BACK MORE.)

-DRAW THE EAR FIRST, & PUT IT BEHIND WHERE THE TWO 'GRID' LINES MEET IN THE MIDDLE FOR A LADY'S EAR ...

(NOTE HOW THE MAN'S EAR GOES MUCH FARTHER BACK...)

-DRAW THE CHIN CURVING UP TO THE
EAR...AND A LONG NECK, WITH TWO LINES..

(SEE HOW THE MAN HAS A BUMP FOR AN
ADAM'S APPLE...

..AND THE MAN OFTEN HAS A FATTER NECK
THAN THE LADY).

-NOW DRAW THE BIG ROUND BACK OVAL OF
THE HEAD, GO ALL AROUND TO REACH THE
FOREHEAD & ADD HAIR. ERASE IF NEEDED
AND REDO. (I ERASED A LOT ON THIS
DRAWING!)

-NEXT DRAW THE FOREHEAD & FACE
OUTLINE. DO IT LIGHTLY AND ERASE IT
UNTIL YOU GET IT LOOKING RIGHT

- NOW DRAW THE EYE-BROW & NOSTRIL
FOR THE NOSE

-LAST, DRAW THE LIPS, UPPER & LOWER FOR HER FACE. (NOTE THERE IS ONLY A LINE FOR THE MAN'S LIPS. BUT SOMETIMES A MAN CAN HAVE FULLER LIPS TOO.)

* * *

I HOPE YOU LIKE IT! HOW DOES IT LOOK?!

NICE WORK!

 IF YOU DO IT TWICE, YOU WILL FIND YOU HAVE LEARNED A LOT ABOUT PLACING FEATURES ON A FACE AND HEAD!

NOW LET'S DRAW A LION FISH ...

THERE ARE ONLY 5 QUICK STEPS!

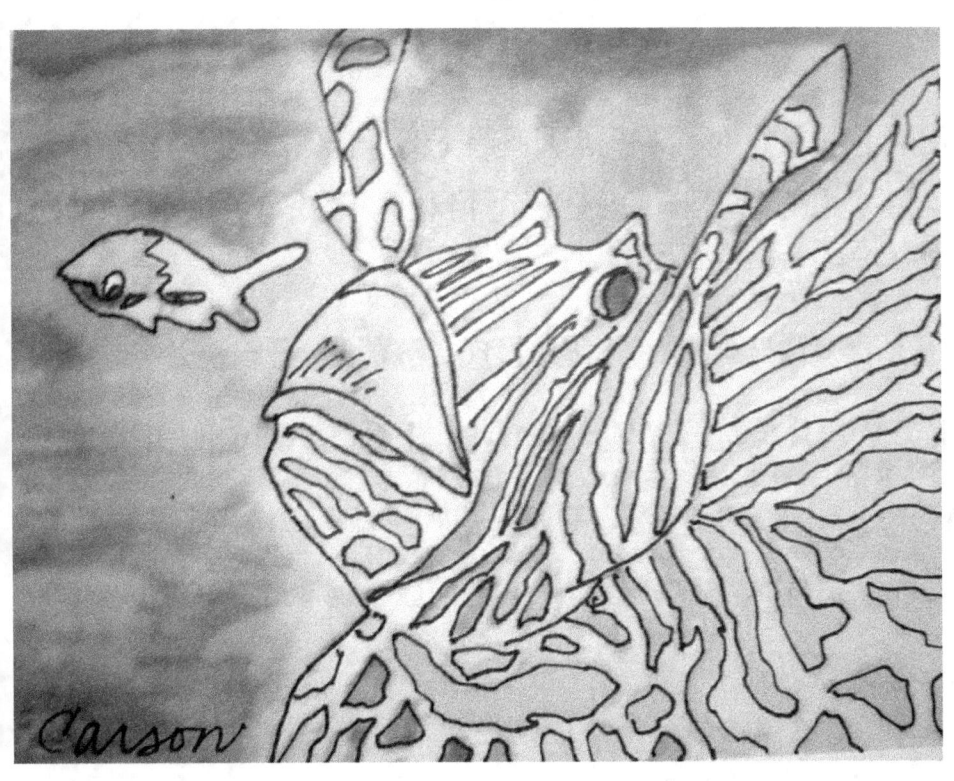

- FIRST, WE WILL DRAW THE BIG OPEN
MOUTH... & THE BABY FISH...!WHY? BECAUSE
THEY ARE THE CENTER OF INTEREST! ..AND
BECAUSE THE BABY FISH IS SOOO CUTE!

- NEXT DRAW THE LIPS...& THE REST OF THE HEAD ...DON'T FORGET THE TOP OF HIS OR HER EYE BUMPS.

- NEXT, DRAW THE BIG OVAL EYE

- NOW DRAW TWO SMALL FINS ON TOP

- ADD ALL THE 'STRIPES' LIKE A TIGER OR ZEBRA HAS... & YOUR LION FISH IS DONE!

GOOD JOB!

* * *

HOW TO DRAW BANANA PLANTS

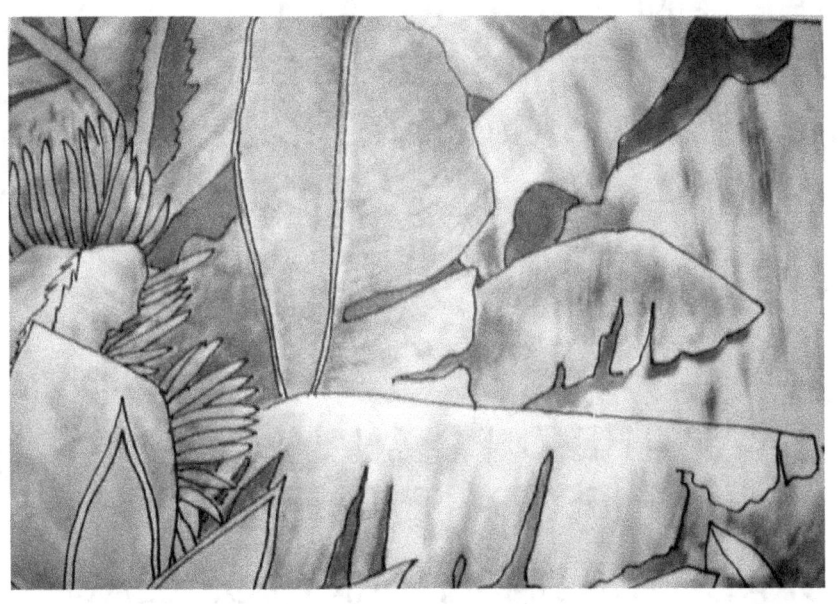

- THERE ARE FOUR LARGE BANANA LEAVES

- 2 BUNCHES OF BANANAS

- AND SOME SMALLER LEAVES TO DRAW.

AND THERE ARE 5 STEPS TO DRAW THEM.

-DRAW THE LONGEST LEAF AT THE BOTTOM, WITH ITS JAGGED EDGES...(THE WIND TEARS THE BIG LEAVES EASILY.)

-NEXT, DRAW THE BIG LEAF THAT STICKS OUT ABOVE IT. SEE IT'S MIDDLE SEAM.

-NOW DRAW THE 3RD AND 4TH BIG LEAF

-NEXT, DRAW THE TINY BANANA FINGERS ON THE 2 BUNCHES...ON THE LEFT SIDE.

-LAST, DRAW THE SMALL PARTS OF LEAVES THAT ARE AROUND THE TINY BANANA FINGERS AND AT THE BOTTOM.

...AND YOUR BANANA PLANT DRAWING IS COMPLETE! WELL DONE!

* * *

HOW TO DRAW A SAIL BOAT ON THE SEA...

HERE ARE SOME KEY PARTS TO DRAW:

MAST – A TALL POLE TO HOLD A SAIL

HULL- SIDES OF THE SHIP

SPRAY - WATER PUSHED UP BY A SHIP or SEA

HORIZON - WATER LINE BEHIND THE SHIP

THERE ARE 7 STEPS TO DRAW THE BOAT:

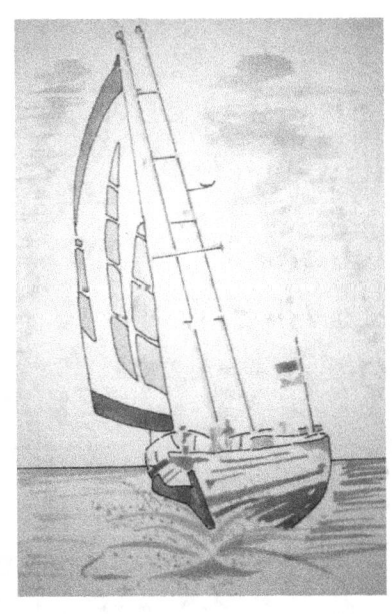

-LET'S DRAW USING PENCIL & A RULER...FIRST DRAW THE HORIZON LINE ACROSS THE PAPER...LOOKING DOWN—IT'S ABOUT 1/3 OF THE WAY TO THE BOTTOM OF THE PAPER

-DRAW 2 LONG, LONG LINES FOR THE 2 BIG MASTS AND 1 LITTLE FLAG POLE..PUT CROSS BARS ON THE MASTS..

-DRAW THE HULL (OR BOTTOM OF THE SHIP)...ITS VERY CURVY SO YOU MAY DO IT AGAIN & ERASE A FEW TIMES TO GET IT JUST RIGHT..PUT THE LINES ALONG THE HULL SIDES TOO...

-DRAW THE BIG TALL SAIL, SHAPED LIKE A FISH...& DRAW THE DESIGNS ON IT...

-NOW DRAW THE BOXES AND SHAPES ON THE DECK OF THE SHIP...SOME ARE TINY PEOPLE...DRAW THE FLAG ON A FLAGPOLE.

-LAST, DRAW THE OCEAN WAVES SPLASHING IN FRONT OF AND BEHIND THE SAILBOAT..

WELL DONE! ITS SAIL-AWAY TIME!

* * *

HOW TO DRAW PLANES

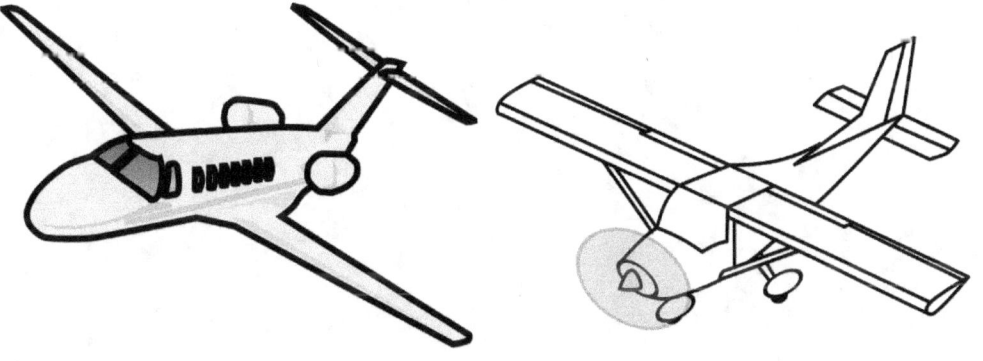

THERE ARE 4 STEPS:

-IN PENCIL, USE A RULER AND DRAW THE WINGS FIRST, THEN THE TAIL.

-NOW DRAW THE NOSE OF THE PLANE AND CONNECT IT TO THE WINGS

-ADD IN A WINDSHIELD, & DRAW THE BODY OF THE PLANE OR 'FUSELAGE'

-DRAW WINDOWS, JET MOTORS, ANY PROPELLER 'CIRCLE' AND WHEELS YOU SEE.

YOUR DRAWING IS DONE! NICE ARTWORK.

* * *

HOW TO DRAW A   BUTTERFLY

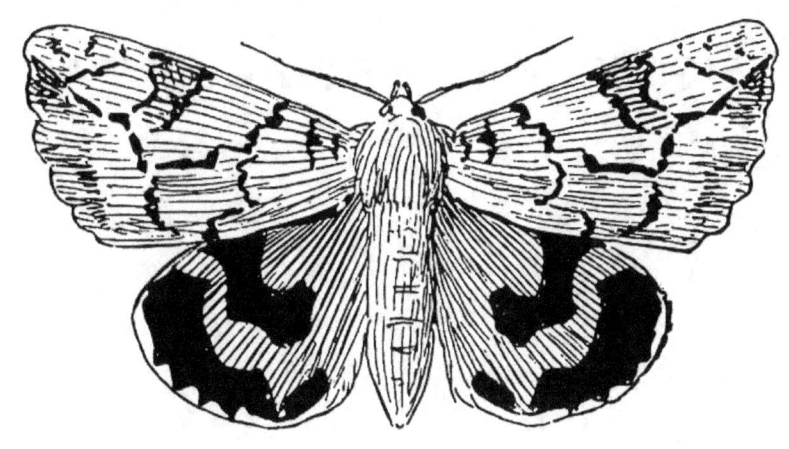

-DRAW IN PENCIL THE BUTTERFLY'S BODY...IT'S LONG AND SORT OF THIN..LOOKS LIKE A WHOLE EAR OF CORN!

-NOW DRAW THE 2 FEELERS OR ANTENNA...ON THE HEAD ... AND DRAW THE TINY HEAD ...

- DRAW THE TWO BIG UPPER WINGS, THEN ADD THE 2 ROUND WINGS BELOW IT...

- NOW, DRAW ALL THE DESIGNS ON IT, MAKE THE PATTERNS AS BUSY OR AS PRETTY AS YOU CAN! YOU MAY WANT TO DRAW A BIGGER ONE, THEN COLOR IT!!

NICELY DONE YOU! * * *

HOW TO DRAW A ROBOT – An easy way to remember in order to draw a robot is:

Body, Legs, Arms and Head...

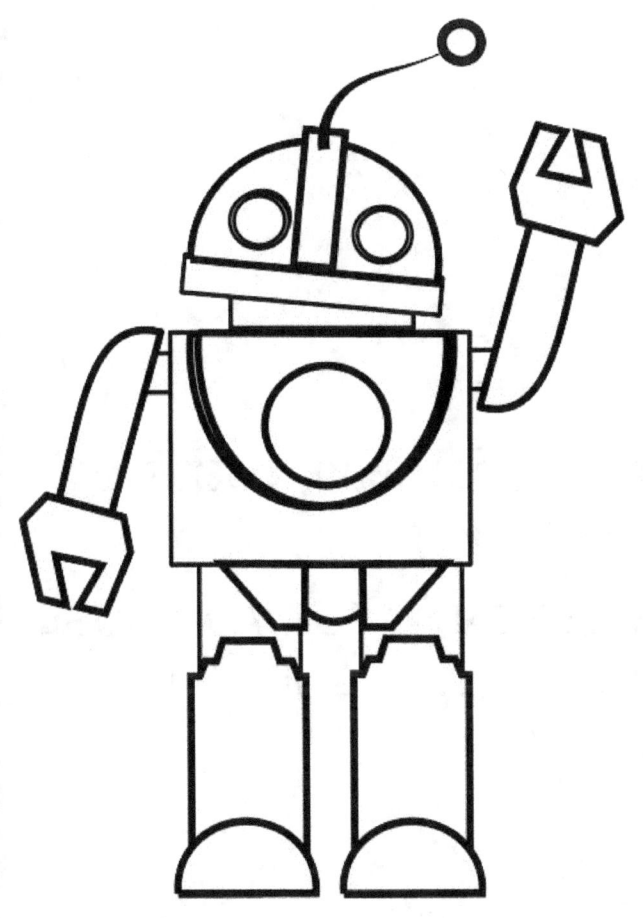

4 STEPS:

-USE A RULER & PENCIL TO DRAW A SQUARE FOR ITS BODY

-DRAW THE LEGS AND PUT BOOTS ON IT

-DRAW   ARMS THAT LOOK LIKE TOOLS FROM A TOOL BENCH ...

-PUT A HALF CIRCLE HEAD ON IT, ADD NOSE, EYES AND ANTENNA....WELL DONE YOU!

* * *

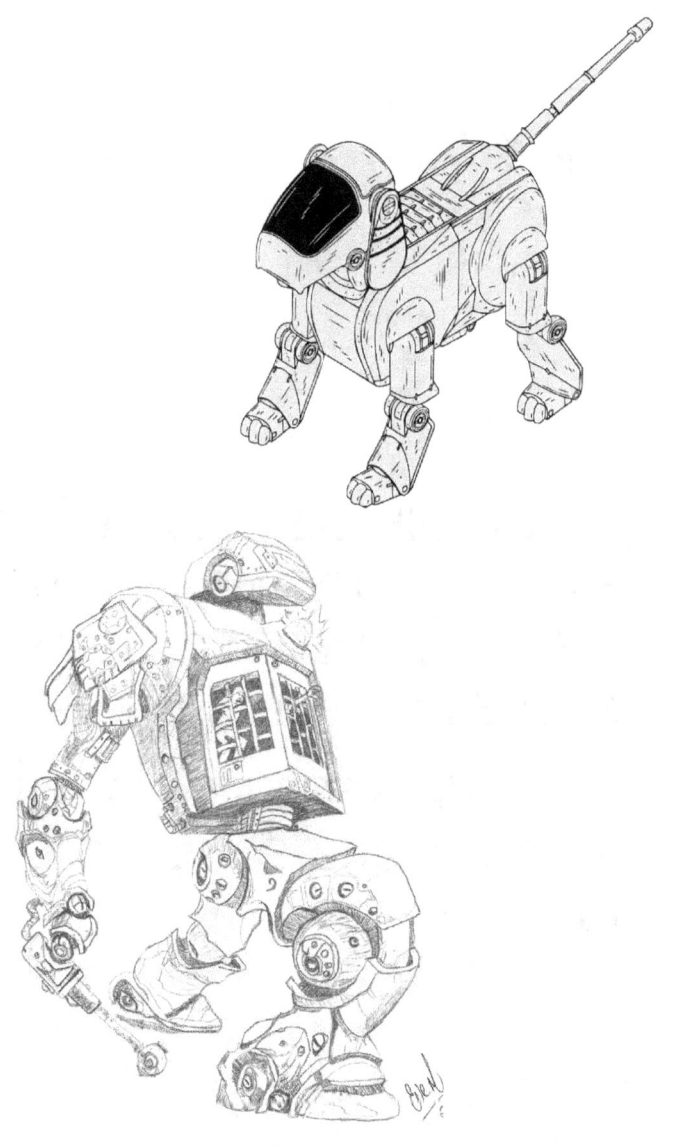

...AND HERE ARE TWO MORE FOR YOU. YOUR ROBOT IS DONE. DOES IT HAVE A NAME?

(AN EASY WAY TO DO ROBOTS IS TO DO...BODY, LEGS & ARMS..THEN HEAD...

THEN PUT IN ALL THE DETAILS LAST...THESE 2 NEW ONES HAVE LOTS MORE DETAIL, BUT YOU USE THE SAME STEPS TO DRAW THEM! ..ADD THE DETAIL LAST.

ROBOT 3 WAS HARD FOR ME TOO, BUT I DID FEWER OF THE BOLTS AND I DID NOT DO THE CAGE!   * * *

TO DRAW A GIRL AND BOY PLAYING

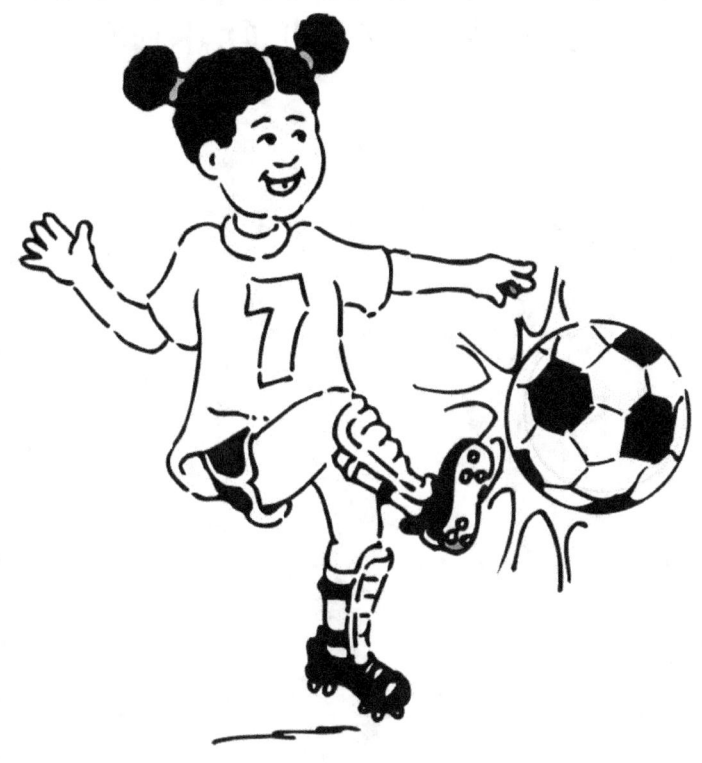

-IN PENCIL, DRAW HER HEAD AND HAIR OUTLINE

-NOW DRAW HER FACE AND HER SMILE

-DRAW HER LEGS AND SHORTS, DON'T BE AFRAID TO ERASE IF THE LEGS ARE TOO LONG OR TOO SHORT OR SKINNY

-LAST, DRAW HER SOCCER SHOES, A SOCCER BALL ... AND DECORATE HER

T-SHIRT. WELL DONE!!

LET'S DRAW THE BOY SKATEBOARDER!

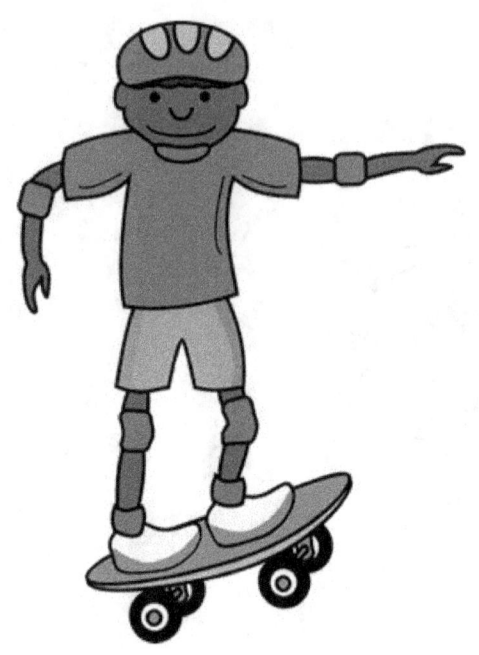

THERE ARE 5 STEPS TO DO IT:

-DRAW IN PENCIL ... THE BOY'S HEAD AND HELMET.

-NEXT, DRAW THE FACE, THE SMILE AND HELMET

-NOW DRAW THE T-SHIRT, ARMS & HANDS

-NOW DRAW THE SHORTS AND LEGS

-LAST, DRAW HIS SHOES & THE SKATE-
BOARD HE'S ON, & DRAW ITS WHEELS!
WELL DONE!

* * *

HOW TO DRAW A CAT

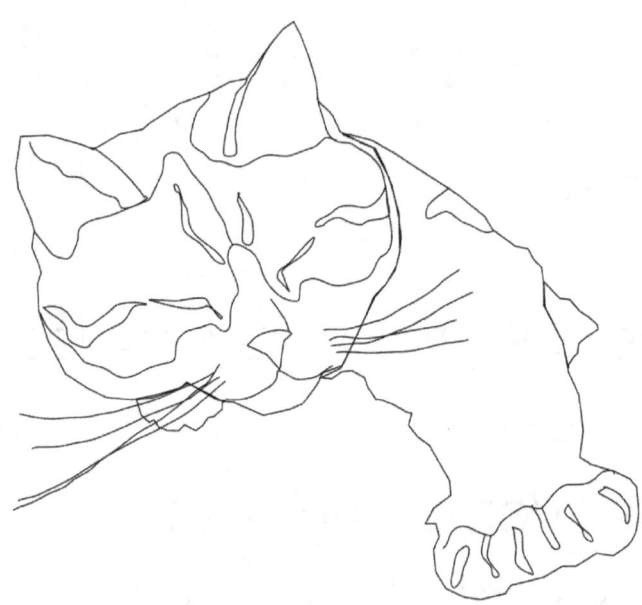

-THE 5 STEPS TO DRAW A LITTLE CAT
ARE:

-IN PENCIL, DRAW THE SORT OF ROUND
AND FLAT HEAD, & ADD 2 POINTY EARS

-DRAW 2 THIN EYES, NOT TOO CLOSE
TOGETHER; DO A TRIANGLE SHAPE FOR A
NOSE

- DRAW THREE LINES FOR THE MOUTH.

- DRAW THE WHISKERS

- THEN DRAW THE FRONT PAW AND...SOME CHEEK LINES

THIS CAT IS SO CUTE! CAN YOU DRAW YOUR CAT?

MAYBE DRAW YOUR CAT ASLEEP! OR TAKE A PICTURE FROM A BOOK OF A CAT AND DRAW IT. THEY DON'T SIT STILL VERY LONG! NICE WORK!

* * *

HOW TO DRAW A CHICKEN OR BIRD...

THE STEPS OF HEAD, BODY, WINGS, FEET..

THESE STEPS WORK FOR ...

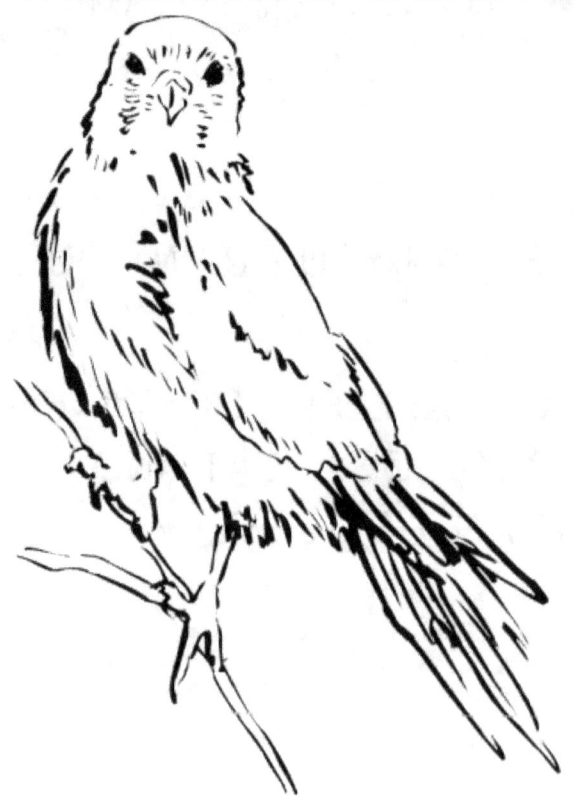

CHICKENS AND BIRDS

DRAW THE CHICKEN:

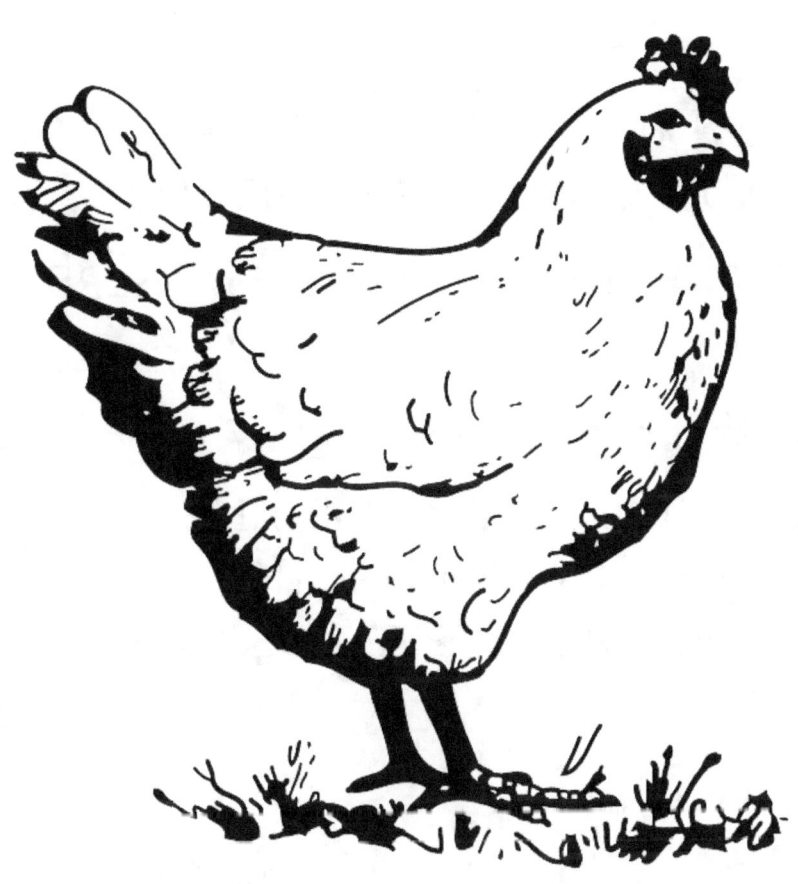

-DRAW   ITS HEAD, IT'S KIND OF SMALL, &
DO THE BEAK AND EYE, AND THE COMB
AROUND THE FACE

-THEN DRAW THE BODY..LUMPY LIKE A
PILLOW, AND BIGGER IN THE MIDDLE.

-NOW ADD THE TAIL OR WING FEATHERS
IN BACK.

-DRAW THE FEET ...

-LAST, ADD SOME FEATHER DETAILS
AROUND THE BODY AND ADD THE GRASS
OR TWIGS UNDER ITS FEET. WELL DONE!!

* * *

YOU CAN EVEN USE THE SAME GUIDE TO
DRAW AN EAGLE

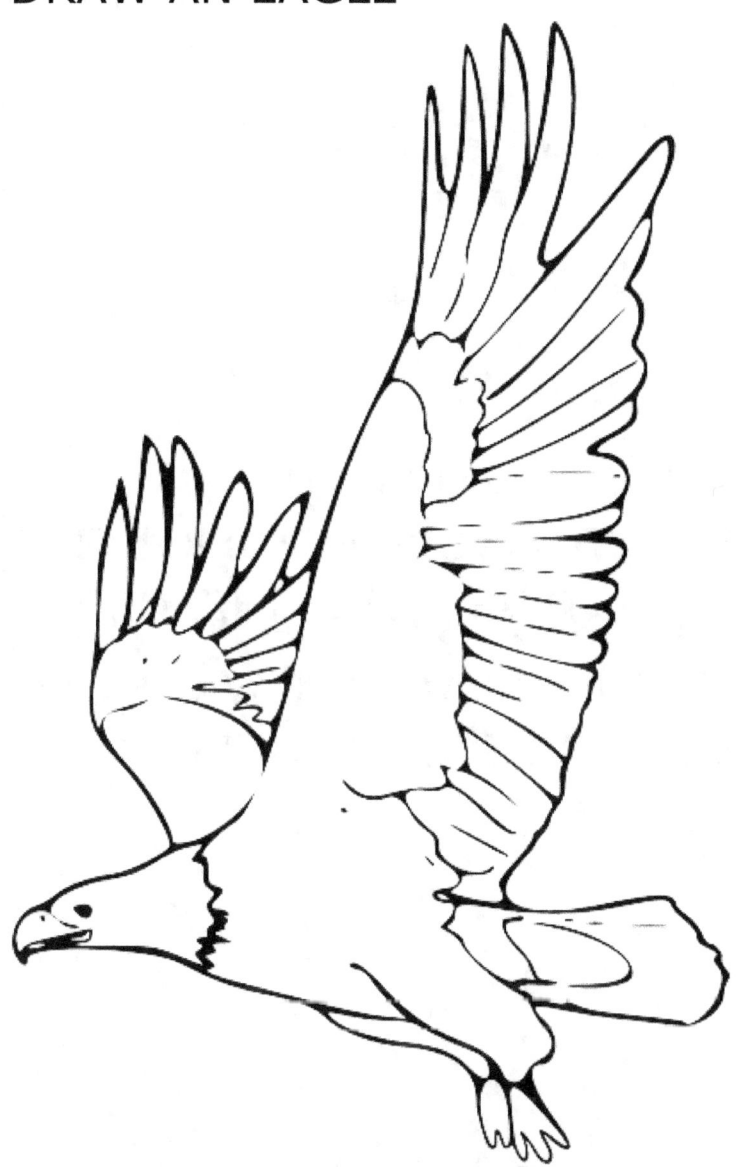

HEAD, BODY, WING FEATHERS, FEET...

VERY NICE JOB! * * *

HOW TO DRAW A FAMOUS ART SCENE...THIS SECTION GIVES SEVERAL FINE ART EXAMPLES TO DRAW, LIKE THIS ONE.

IT'S FROM EDVARD MUNCH...HE WAS FROM NORWAY. HE WAS A MODERN ARTIST.

DRAW THE SCREAM...

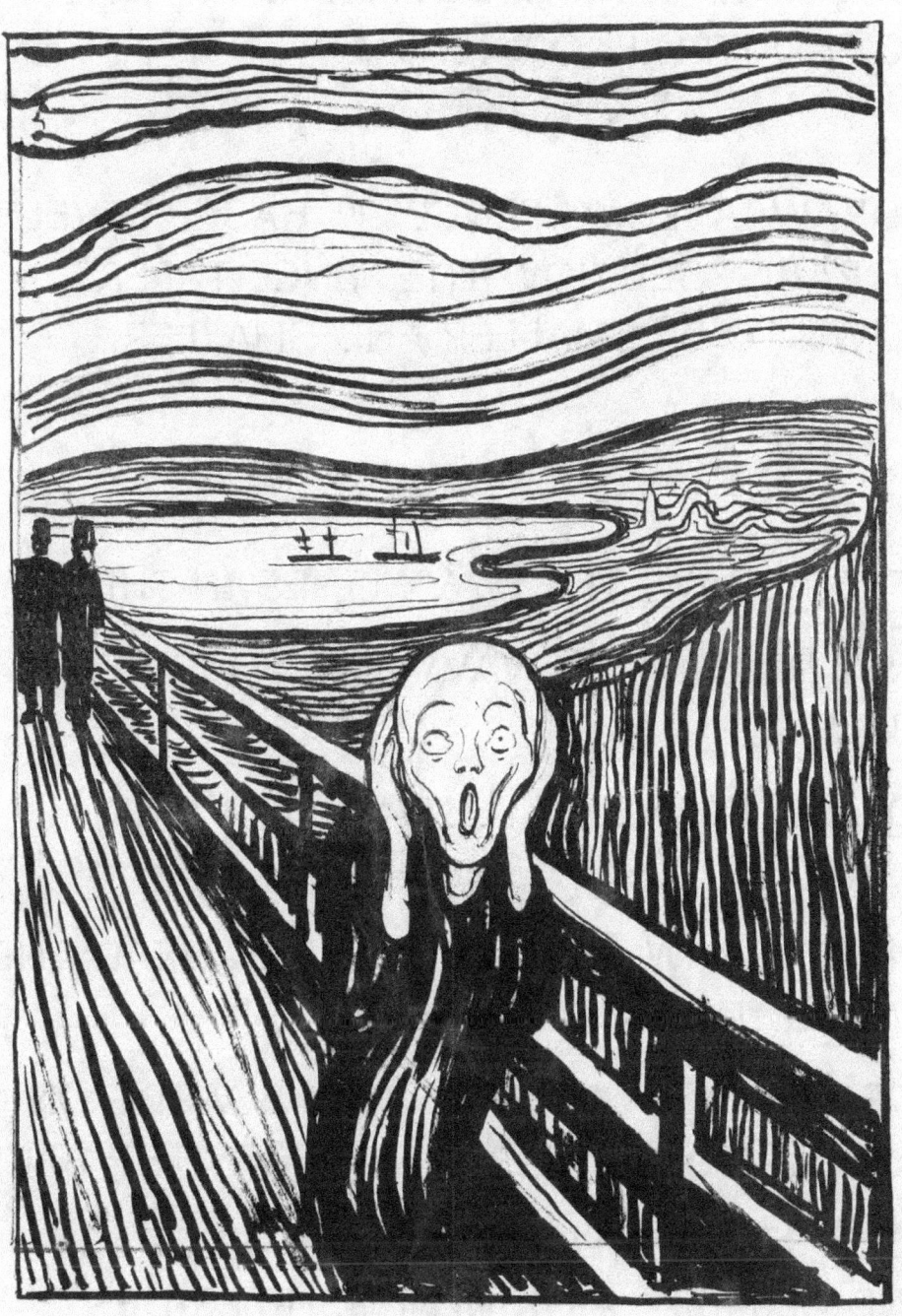

-USE A PENCIL & RULER AND DRAW THE BOXY OUTLINE OR FRAME

- DRAW A LONG FENCE...IT HAS 3 LEVELS OF RAILS. SEE HOW THE FENCE TAPERS DOWN TO BE SMALLER AND SMALLER...

-THEN DRAW THE WAVY LINES IN THE SKY.

-NET DRAW THE WAVY LINE FOR THE HILLS

-DRAW IN THE LITTLE LAKE, & 2 TINY BOATS.

-NEXT DRAW THE SCARY GUY'S HEAD AND HANDS. THEN ADD HIS BODY.

-DRAW THE PLANKS OF THE BOARDS ON THE WALKWAY, & 2 TINY MEN AT THE BACK.

-LAST, DRAW ALL THE LINES FOR GRASS AND CLIFFS... AROUND THE HILLSIDES..

HOW DID YOU DO? DO YOU LIKE IT?
WELL DONE!!!

* * *

HOW TO DRAW A STARRY NIGHT

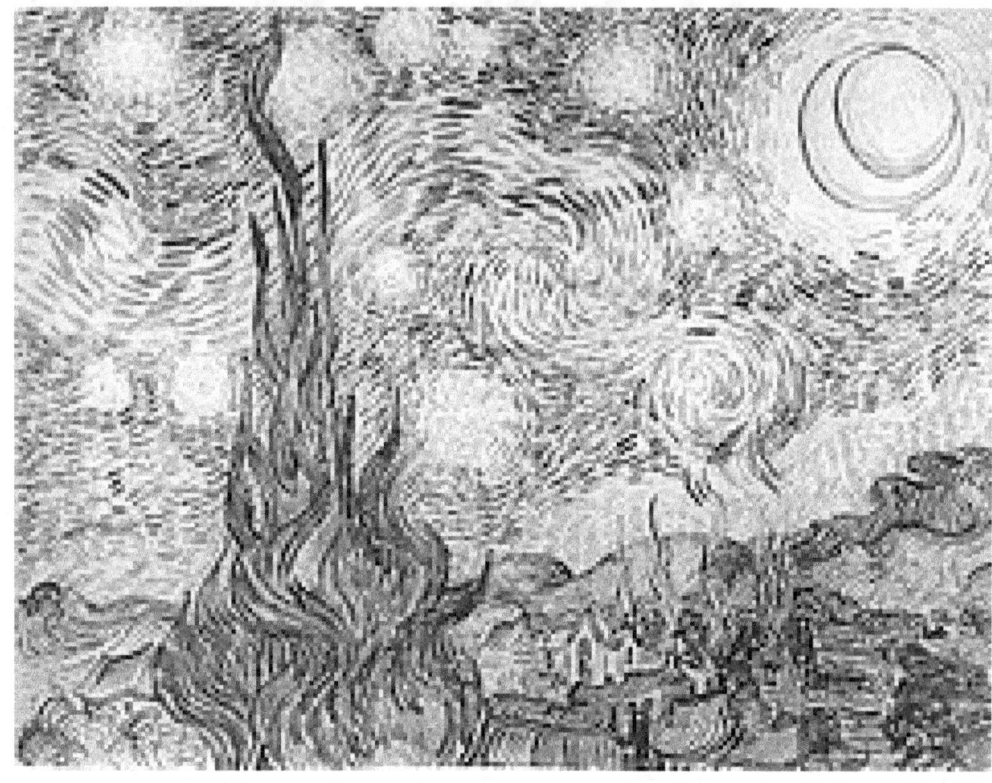

THIS DRAWING IS OF A FAMOUS PAINTING
BY DUTCH PAINTER VINCENT VAN GOGH..IT
HAS THE MOON SHINING WITH 11 BRIGHT
STARS ...ON A STARRY NIGHT. HE USED
BOTH A FULL MOON AND CRESCENT
MOON!

WE ARE GOING TO DRAW A STARRY NIGHT...IN 6 EASY STEPS.

BECAUSE VAN GOGH MADE LOTS & LOTS OF BIG & BOLD DASHES & LINES, YOU MAY WANT TO DRAW THIS ONE... USING YOUR CRAYONS OR MARKERS... PENCILS WORK TOO...AND YOU CAN ERASE!

HOW TO DRAW 'STARRY NIGHT:'

-FIRST, DRAW THE 'CRESCENT' MOON UP IN THE CORNER OF THE SKY... AND PUT SOME SWIRLY CIRCLES AROUND IT.

-DRAW THE LAND BELOW THE SKY, AND DRAW THE LITTLE CHURCH & BIG TREE THAT'S IN THE BOTTOM CORNER...

-THERE ARE 11 ROUND STARS IN THE SKY, WITH LINES SWIRLING AROUND EACH STAR... DRAW THE STARS & ALL THE SWIRLS...

-LAST, ON THE HILLS AT THE BOTTOM, DO LIKE VAN GOGH DID. HE DREW LOTS OF

DASH-LIKE LINES TO INDICATE ALL THE FIELDS ON THE SIDES OF THE HILLS.

-YOU CAN MAKE YOUR STARRY NIGHT A MIXED MEDIA DRAWING. DRAW IT FIRST IN PENCIL, AND WHEN YOU HAVE COMPLETED IT, GO BACK OVER WITH MARKER OR INK...

THIS MAKES IT'S LINES IN THE DRAWING STAND OUT MORE! WELL DONE!

VanGogh tried to be a preacher, like his father, but he was too shy to speak in public. So he became a painter instead, to offer his talent to God in his artwork. But he was very poor...and not a very successful artist when he was alive.   But today his art is worth millions of dollars!! SO sad he did not live to see it.

* * *

HOW TO DRAW A PAUL KLEE ABSTRACT:

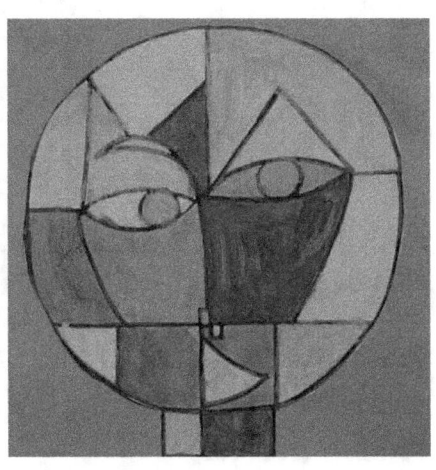

-TO DRAW AN ABSTRACT WORK LIKE PAUL KLEE...FIRST MAKE A BIG CIRCLE ..& ADD A NECK.

-NEXT, DRAW TWO EYES AND PUT SOME TRIANGLES AROUND THEM. DRAW EYES..THEN DRAW THE CHEEKS UNDER THE EYES.

-DRAW A LINE WITH A RULER ACROSS THE MOUTH AREA, AND PUT IN SOME CUBES BELOW THE LINE

-DRAW THE CHIN, (A WEDGE) , AND TWO TINY LIPS. AND SHADE IN SOME OF THE SQUARES.... YOUR CUBIST ART IS DONE!

-KLEE WAS A CUBIST PAINTER LIKE PICASSO. THEY USED FEW BUT BIG BOLD OFTEN CUBE-LIKE DETAILS. ABSTRACT ARTWORK LIKE HIS IS FUN TO DO! YOU CAN GO WILD!!!

* * *

TWO BEARS DANCE

This drawing is in the style of Keith Haring.
His art is a type of 'Pop Art" that is easy on
the eyes and playful. A version of this pair of
bears done in orange color is a large painting
Haring did for Elton John, the song artist.

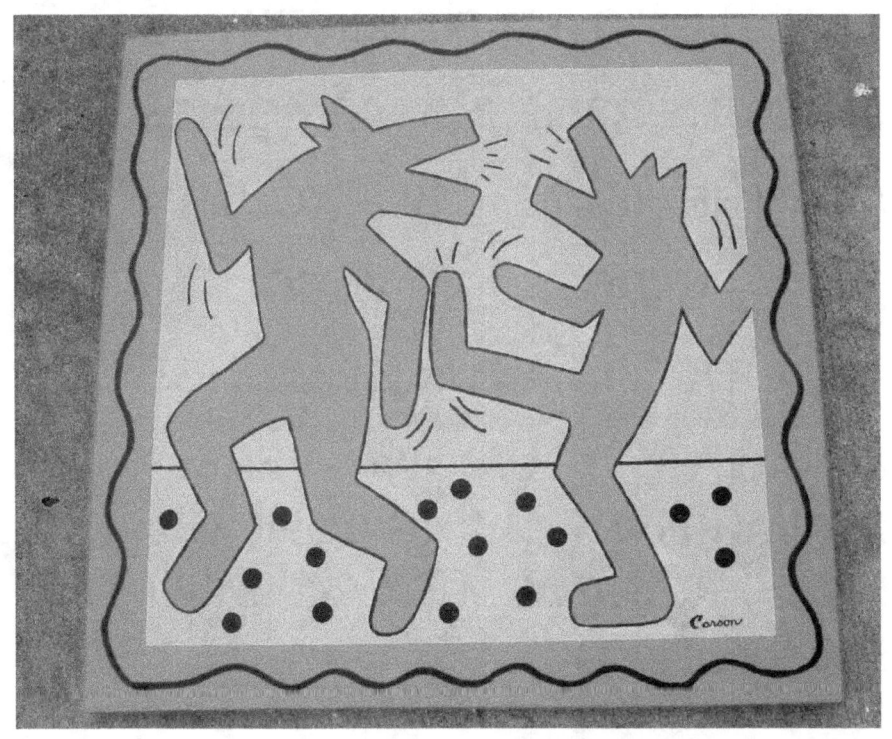

-TO DO DANCING BEARS, DRAW A FRAME
AROUND YOUR PAPER.

-THEN, DRAW THE WAVY LINE AROUND THE
FRAME.

-DRAW A LINE FOR THE DANCE FLOOR.

-NOW DRAW THE FEET & LEGS OF THE BEARS. (I HAD TO ERASE A LOT!!)

-NEXT, DO THE ARMS & BEAR BODIES.

-NOW DO THE HEADS & BIG MOUTHS

-LAST, DO THE DOTS AND WIGGLE MARKS!

NICE JOB! THIS IS A FUN DRAWING!!

TRY TO CREATE YOUR OWN VERSION OF DANCING ANIMALS, USING SOME OF HARING'S ART IDEAS. HE WAS VERY CLEVER! GOOD JOB!

* * *

DRAW LIKE A PICASSO...WORLD FAMOUS MODERN ARTIST... $185 MILLON WAS PAID FOR ONE OF HIS PAINTINGS...

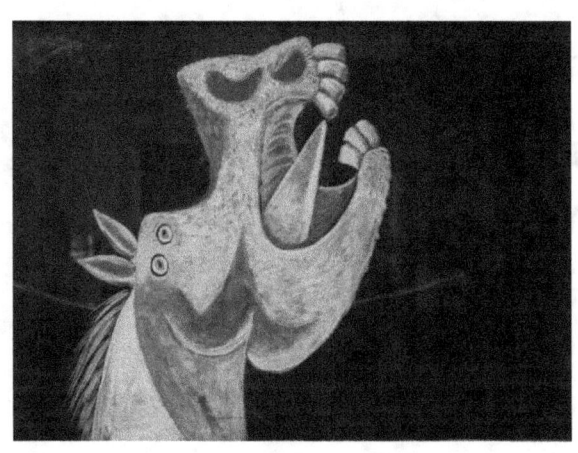

DRAW A HORSE THAT IS ANGRY, LIKE THIS PICASSO HORSE, IN 5 STEPS

-DRAW THE MOUTH OF THE HORSE FIRST, AS IT IS THE CENTER OF INTEREST.

-DRAW THE SHARP TONGUE & 7 TEETH

-NEXT, DRAW THE NOSE, ITS REALLY BIG AND HAS BIG NOSTRILS

-DRAW THE FACE, ITS EYES & EARS

-DRAW THE LOWER JAW, BIG & ROUND

-ADD THE NECK, THE MANE AND IT'S DONE! IT IS DRAWN IN A CUBIST STYLE, LIKE PICASSO. ERASE WHEN NEEDED.

NICE!

You may ask why the horse was angry? Picasso was upset that the War in Spain, where he lived, damaged a nearby village, Guernica. He painted this, partly, to vent his own anger.

* * *

HOW TO DRAW AN OCEAN WAVE, LIKE
HOKUSAI:

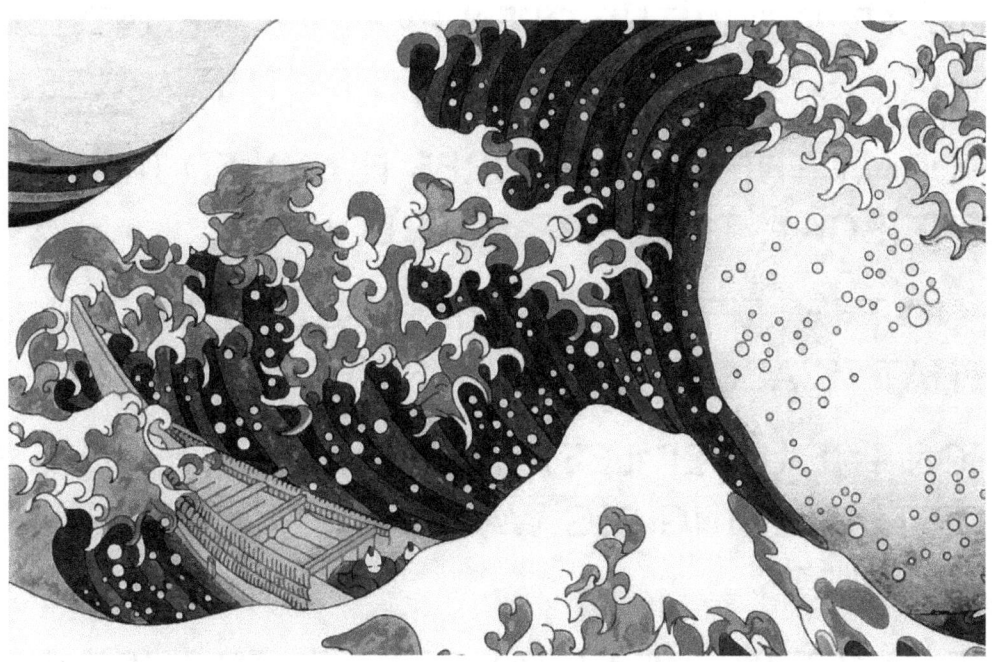

HOKUSAI WAS A PAINTER FROM JAPAN
LONG AGO. HE LOVED TO PAINT THE
OCEAN. THIS IS A DETAIL OF HIS
ARTWORK.

-OBSERVE HOW SOME WAVES ARE ALL
BREAKING AT THE SAME TIME...

THERE ARE 7 STEPS TO DO THIS SEASCAPE:

-LET'S DRAW THE FIRST BIG WAVE ON THE BOTTOM THAT IS RISING UP, AND ADD DETAILS, LIKE ALL ITS WAVELET CURLS.

-NEXT, DRAW THE OPEN PART OF A BOAT THAT IS GETTING SWAMPED BY THE WAVES

–DRAW THE TWO FIGURES HUDDLED INSIDE THE BOAT..THEY ARE SCARED!

-ON THE LEFT, DRAW THE WAVE OF WATER THAT IS ABOUT TO FILL THE BOAT

-ON THE UPPER LEFT, NOW DRAW THE TOP OF THE RISING BIG WAVE, & MANY, MANY WAVELETS

-DRAW THE SEA-SPRAY CIRCLES IN THE AIR

-LAST, DRAW THE BIG UPPER WAVE, & PUT THE RISING OCEAN WATER LINES AND AS

MUCH WAVLET DETAIL & SPRAY AS YOU CAN..THIS IS A VERY POWERFUL IMAGE OF OCEAN WAVES...WELL DONE YOU!

* * *

I HOPE YOU HAVE ENJOYED THE DRAWING
IDEAS HERE, AND HAVE SOME NEW IDEAS
OF YOUR OWN OF THINGS AND PEOPLE AND
PLACES YOU WANT TO DRAW. HAVE FUN!

I HAD FUN WRITING THIS BOOK TOO!

By Margaret Carson

WELL DONE YOU!!

CONCLUSIONS:

I hope that you have enjoyed drawing and seeing some of the ideas in this book. Most of all, I hope your skills in observing things around us that we may wish to draw have become more sensitive and useful. We have considered where the light on an object may come from, like the apple or the hibiscus flower.

We have thought about what is at the base of our drawing, like the branch supporting the frog or the wave supporting Hokusai's little boat.   We have learned about use of the grid to help us place people and things in position better.

We have thought about leaving plenty of room on our drawing paper so the whole panda bear or all of the soccer girl will fit.

We have learned its okay to erase, erase, erase too to help get our drawing right!

Create your own ideas like VanGogh, Picasso
and Haring did!   Enjoy drawing for fun.

THANK YOU.   By Margaret Carson

* * *

MARGARET CARSON –

BIOGRAPHY – 2021

Margaret Carson holds a Bachelor of Arts degree from University of Pittsburgh in 1975 and attended Houston Baptist University where she earned a Masters of Arts degree in 1985. She studied art, painting, fine arts and drawing at Carnegie Art Institute in Pittsburgh from 1975 to 1980. She also studied art at Glassell School of Art in Houston, at Rice University and the Houston Art League. She is the author of "Artful Watercolor Techniques," and "ARTFUL COLORS," "ARTFUL STILL LIFE," and "MODERN ART" published as an ebook and in print by Amazon Digital Printing. She teaches painting and drawing on various cruise lines, including Royal Caribbean, Celebrity, Cunard, Princess and Azamara...and looks forward to sailing again soon, when covid goes away.

She is a painter and lecturer on art and the lives of the Masters. Her paintings are classic in style and developed with a strong sense of the impressionist school. She has taught seascape and landscape painting and drawing and lectures on impressionism, the lives of the Fine Artists and watercolor painting, drawing and color theory to classes and audiences in the US and abroad. She is married to artist and painter Brian Scruby. Her art is inspired by the beautiful works of Van Gogh, Monet, Matisse and Cezanne.

She has exhibited her artworks at various galleries and art exhibitions in the United States, South America and abroad. She was selected as Outstanding Artist by Molgaard Galleries in Sweden. Her paintings are located in private collections in the United States, Central and South America and in Europe. Her paintings are also shown in the

US in bricks-and-mortar and online galleries at www.yourart.com and www.fineartamerica.com .

   You can email the artist at: mcarson8888@comcast.net

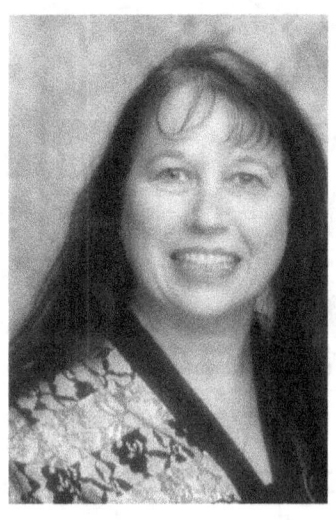

Margaret Carson

* * *

ACKNOWLEDGEMENTS

Margaret Carson wishes to thank her wonderful husband and artist, Brian Scruby, for his tremendous technical and artistic support and unwavering assistance in accomplishing this Artful Drawing for Children book. He is the artist and photographer helping contribute many of the wonderful images and paintings.

She also wishes to thank her sister and friend, Joan Maune, for her valuable commentary and reviews of text and proofreading of this book. She wishes to also thank her friend and author Joanne Weck, noted mystery novel writer, for her clever commercial and creative guidance. Thanks to Etsy, Wikimedia, Microsoft, and pixabay. Thank you to Claire Kabala, for her guidance and editing from the youthful artist point of view and thanks to Jack Kabala for his ideas.

Without the help, patience and dedication to this book of each of these individuals and services, this book would not have been possible.

Thank you all so much! Happy drawing!

MARGARET CARSON

* * *